Learn and Spell

26 Letters of Power

Frank-N and Dotsie j

WestBow Press books may be ordered through booksellers or by contacting:

WestBow Press
A Division of Thomas Nelson
1663 Liberty Drive
Bloomington, IN 47403
www.westbowpress.com
1-(866) 928-1240

Because of the dynamic nature of the Internet, any web addresses or links contained in this book may have changed since publication and may no longer be valid. The views expressed in this work are solely those of the author and do not necessarily reflect the views of the publisher, and the publisher hereby disclaims any responsibility for them.

Any people depicted in stock imagery provided by Thinkstock are models, and such images are being used for illustrative purposes only.

Certain stock imagery © Thinkstock.

ISBN: 978-1-4497-4417-5

Library of Congress Control Number: 2012905270

Printed in the United States of America

WestBow Press rev. date: 4/24/2012

WESTBOW
PRESS

"Train up a child in the way he should go: and when he is old, he will not depart from it". Proverbs (22:6) (KJV)

This Book is dedicated to the love ones in our life:

Dorthine, Tyra, Demetroius, My Dad Frank-O, Jit, my chidren Lowen, Suani

and Pamela also all my grand / great grand children down the line.

Speacal Thanks to our mothers, and the lord Jesus Christ who

guided our hands for the seven years it took to complete this book. Thanks!

Frank-N and Dotsie j

A Is the letter number # 1   **B** Is the letter number # 2

Jesus loves me and you.

C Is the letter number # 3   **D** Is the letter number # 4

knock, knock, Jesus Christ is at the door.

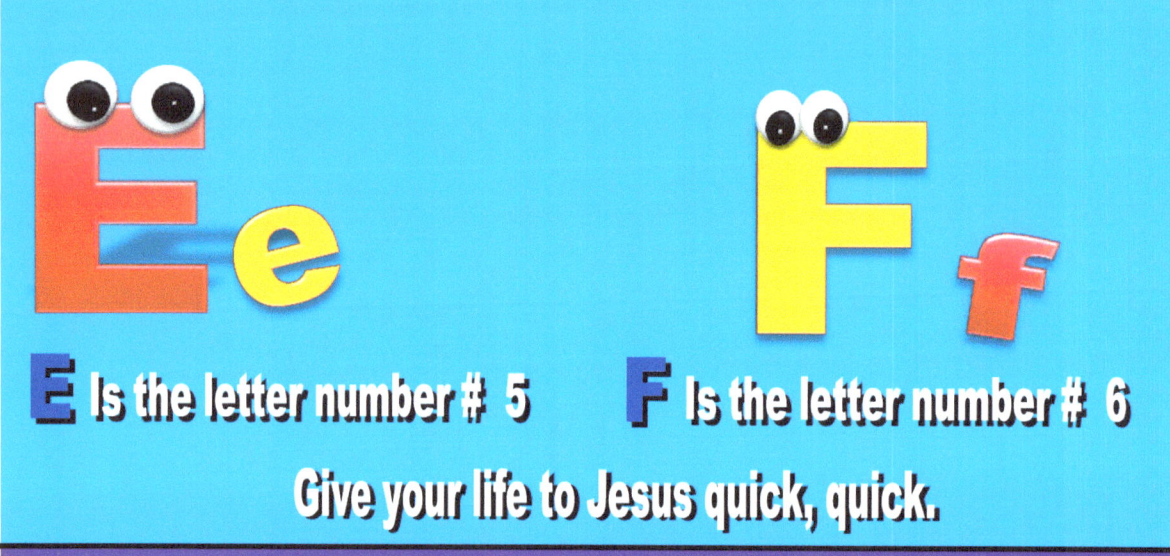

E Is the letter number # 5

F Is the letter number # 6

Give your life to Jesus quick, quick.

G Is the letter number # 7

H Is the letter number # 8

We all know **GOD** is great.

I Is the letter number # 9 **J** Is the letter number # 10

I know your going to win.

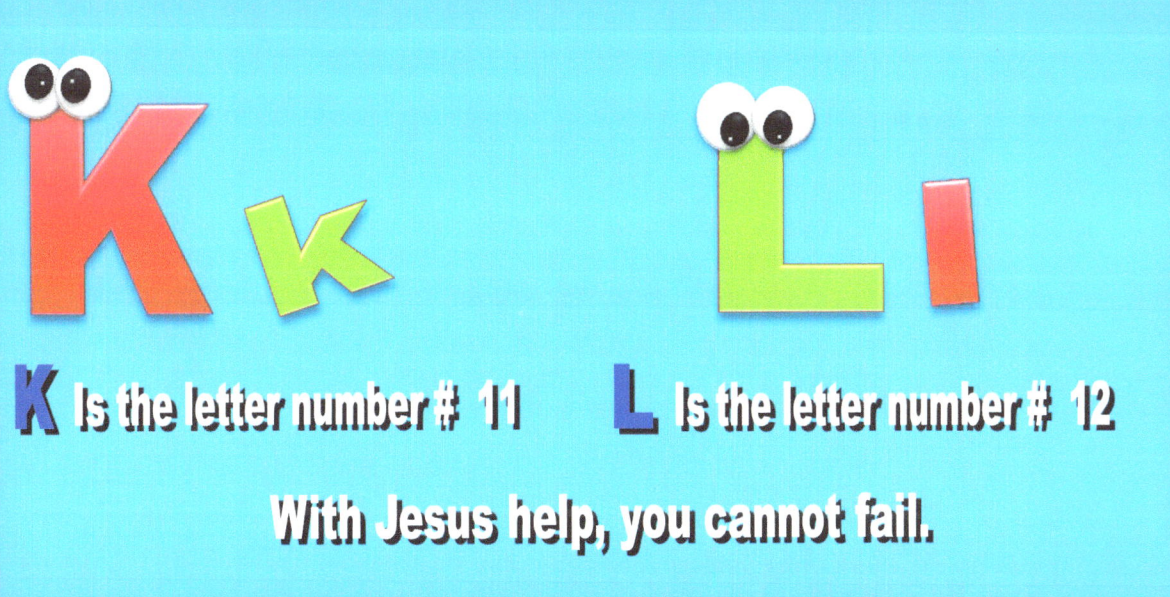

K Is the letter number # 11 **L** Is the letter number # 12

With Jesus help, you cannot fail.

M Is the letter number # 13   **N** Is the letter number # 14

Thank God for everything.

O Is the letter number # 15   **P** Is the letter number # 16

Joy, joy Jesus will bring.

Q Is the letter number # 17   **R** Is the letter number # 18

Be happy happy and sing, sing, sing.

S Is the letter number # 19   **T** Is the letter number # 20

Jesus helps many, many.

U Is the letter number # 21   **V** Is the letter number # 22

Hold on your almost through.

W Is the letter number # 23   **X** Is the letter number # 24

You can do it there's only two more.

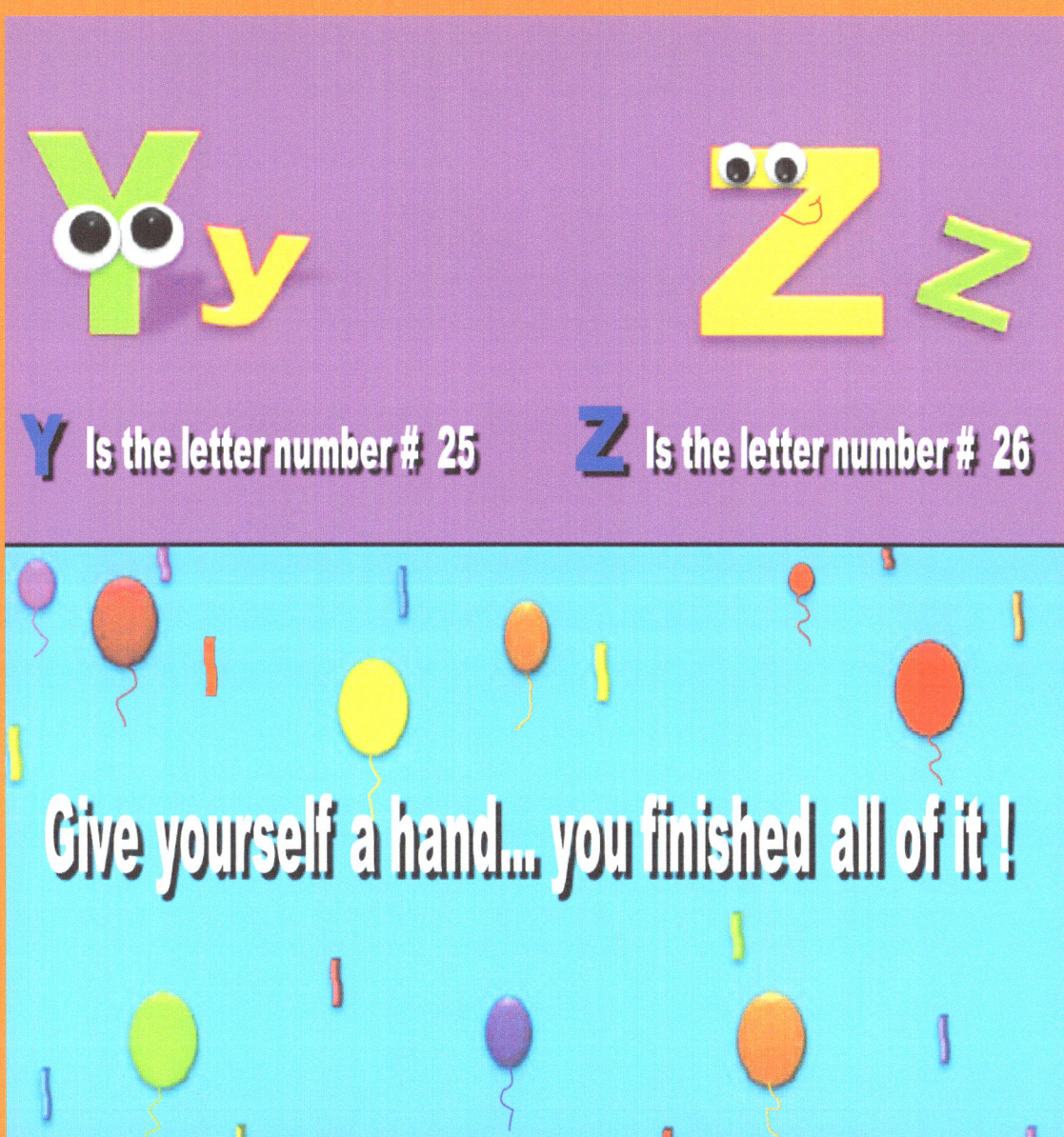

LEARN AND SPELL CHARACTERS

LEARN AND SPELL CHARACTERS

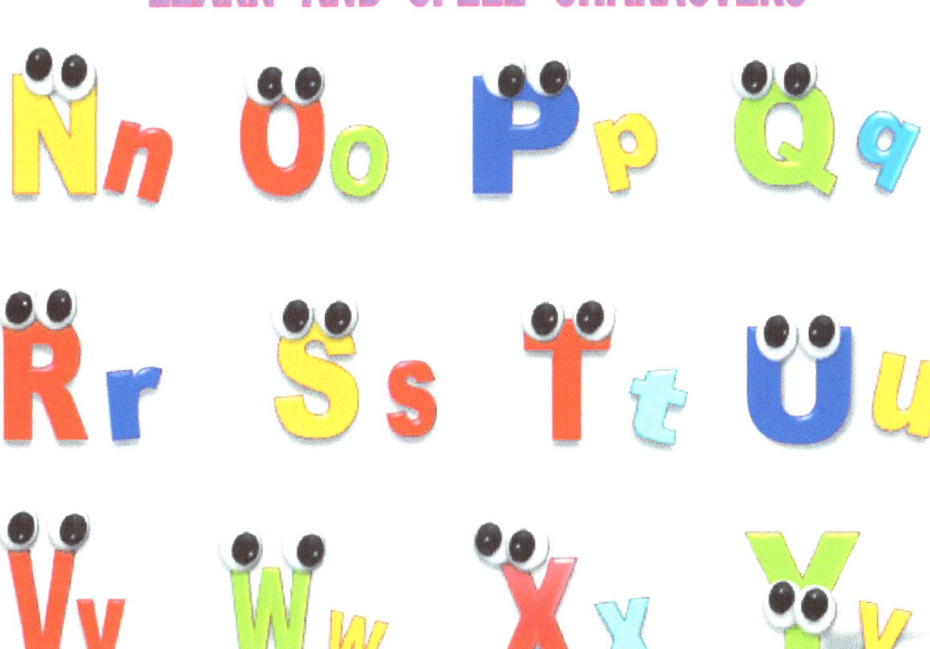

Nn Oo Pp Qq
Rr Ss Tt Uu
Vv Ww Xx Yy

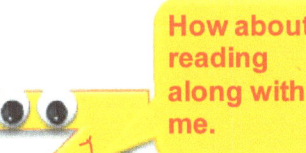

How about reading along with me.

Zz

JOHN 3:16 (KJV)

FOR GOD SO LOVED THE WORLD THAT HE GAVE HIS ONLY BEGOTTEN SON, THAT WHOSOEVER BELIEVETH IN HIM SHOULD NOT PERISH BUT HAVE EVERLASTING LIFE.

JESUS LOVES YOU
ROMANS 10:9-15

How to play

1. Write in the missing letters or numbers.

A	B	C	D	E	F	G
a	b	c	d	e	f	g
1	2	3	4	5	6	7

H	I	J	K	L	M	N
h	i	j	k	l	m	n
8	9	10	11	12	13	14

O	P	Q	R	S	T	U
o	p	q	r	s	t	u
15	16	17	18	19	20	21

V	W	X	Y	Z
v	w	x	y	z
22	23	24	25	26

2. Use a timer, or play against a friend.

3. Your challenge is to show mom, dad or a teacher that you can memorize and write each alphabet's number by yourself.

4. It's ok if you forget, simply look at this page again, the answer is in there for you.

Fil - Lit

YOU CAN DO IT!

	B		D			G
a		c		e	f	
1			4		6	

Write in the missing letters or numbers.

Fil 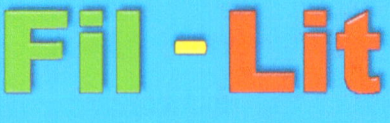 - Lit

Two pages to go!

H		J			M	
	i		k	l		n
8		10		12		

Write in the missing letters or numbers.

Fil - Lit

J

One page to go!

	P		R			U
o			r	s		
		17			20	

Write in the missing letters or numbers.

Fil -Lit

you did it!

J

	W			Z
v		x	y	
	23		25	

Write in the missing letters or numbers.

Fil -Lit

Wecome to level 2...

Q		X		S	B	T
q	i		d	s		
	9		4			20

Write in the missing letters or numbers.

Fil - Lit

Two pages left keep going!

	E	Z		A	P	
m		z	j		p	h
	5		10			

Write in the missing letters or numbers.

Fil - Lit

Great Job only one left!

Write in the missing letters or numbers.

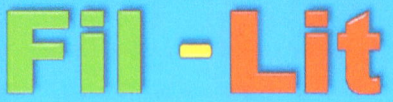

Fil -Lit

you made it, good good job!

F		R		
f		r	u	k
	22		21	

Write in the missing letters or numbers.

How to play

THE NUMFABETS GAME

1. Match each alphabet to it's number home.

2. Use a timer, or play against a friend.

3. Your challenge is to show mom, dad or a teacher that you can memorize each alphabet's number by yourself.

4. It's ok if you forget, simply read your book again, the answer is in there for you.

For questions or comments email us: learnandspell@usa.com